Brian Fleming Research & Learning Library
Ministry of Education
Ministry of Training, Colleges & Universities
900 Bay St. 13th Floor, Mowat Block
Toronto, ON M7A 1L2

The HBR List

The HBR List

Breakthrough Ideas for 2009

Harvard Business Press

Boston, Massachusetts

Copyright 2009 Harvard Business School Publishing Corporation
All rights reserved
Printed in the United States of America
13 12 11 10 09   5 4 3 2 1

No part of this publication may be reproduced, stored in or introduced into a retrieval system, or transmitted, in any form, or by any means (electronic, mechanical, photocopying, recording, or otherwise), without the prior permission of the publisher. Requests for permission should be directed to permissions@hbsp.harvard.edu, or mailed to Permissions, Harvard Business School Publishing, 60 Harvard Way, Boston, Massachusetts 02163.

ISBN-13: 978-1-4221-4760-3

Contents

1 Consumer Safety for Consumer Credit
   BY ELIZABETH WARREN AND AMELIA TYAGI

6 Now's the Time to Invest in Africa
   BY PAUL COLLIER AND JEAN-LOUIS WARNHOLZ

10 Just Because I'm Nice, Don't Assume I'm Dumb
   BY AMY J. C. CUDDY

14 Forget Citibank—Borrow from Bob
   BY JOHN SVIOKLA

17 Harnessing Social Pressure
   BY NOAH J. GOLDSTEIN

20 The Rise of Forensic Economics
BY RAYMOND FISMAN

24 A Looming American Diaspora
BY PAUL SAFFO

27 Institutional Memory Goes Digital
BY GURDEEP SINGH PALL AND RITA GUNTHER MCGRATH

30 The Business of Biomimicry
BY JANINE M. BENYUS AND GUNTER A.M. PAULI

35 The IKEA Effect: When Labor Leads to Love
BY MICHAEL I. NORTON

38 Beware Global Cooling
BY PETER SCHWARTZ

41 The Dynamics of Personal Influence

BY NICHOLAS A. CHRISTAKIS

44 Western Union World

BY MARCELO SUAREZ-OROZCO

47 State Capitalism Makes a Comeback

BY IAN BREMMER AND JUAN PUJADAS

52 Launching a Better Brain

BY STEVE JURVETSON

55 Stumbling to a Longer Life

BY LEW MCCREARY

58 What You Need to Know About the Semantic Web

BY TOM ILUBE

62 How Social Networks Network Best
BY ALEX PENTLAND

66 Should You Outsource Your Brain?
BY THOMAS H. DAVENPORT AND BALA IYER

70 A Central Nervous System for the Earth
BY R. STANLEY WILLIAMS

Note

You hold in your hands a snapshot of the emerging shape of business in 2009 and beyond.

Each year, the editors of *Harvard Business Review* consult their extensive network of expert authors to identify the best ideas that will likely influence the future of business. For the 2009 List, the editors also took part in a day-long brainstorming session with the World Economic Forum, which surfaced many of the new ideas that led to this year's selections.

The 2009 List aims to encompass those ideas that seem most vital for the immediate future. Because many of these concepts originated months ago, the editors did their best to anticipate the context in which you now read them. In keeping with the current business climate, this year's ideas tend to be more useful than fanciful, more immediately practicable than speculative. However, while some of the articles you'll find here comment directly on the economic crisis that escalated late in 2008, most address matters that business leaders must contend with every day. Among these, you'll find articles covering the best new thinking on: strategic decision making, tapping new markets, finding and keeping top talent, harnessing network effects, and dealing with disruptive technologies and business models.

We hope this year's List leaves you not only with a better sense of what issues and opportunities await business on the horizon, but also new tools and concepts that can help you get ahead of the curve today.

Consumer Safety for Consumer Credit

> Laws and regulations guarantee the basic safety of every product sold in the United States—except consumer credit instruments. The lack of such protections for the holders of credit cards, auto loans, and mortgages contributed to the financial crisis. The authors argue that credit cards can and should be made as consumer friendly as toasters.

By Elizabeth Warren and Amelia Tyagi

In all the finger-pointing during the financial meltdown, one major culprit was largely overlooked: the legal structure governing the sale of mortgages, credit cards, and other consumer financial products.

Unlike most consumer purchases, consumer credit in the United States is still grounded firmly in eighteenth-century contract law. In 2009 the basic premise is what it was in rural England in 1709—two merchants might dicker over the terms of an agreement, and the courts would enforce whatever they decided. The principle of caveat emptor ruled—anyone who bought goods was stuck with them, no matter their defects and no matter the injury they might cause. This approach made a certain amount of sense for two small-business owners bargaining over the sale of a plow. Government's responsibility wasn't to protect consumers from dangerous products but to enforce contracts and keep the wheels of commerce moving smoothly.

Today, however, caveat emptor has disappeared. The Consumer Product Safety Commission (CPSC) ensures the basic safety of every type of product sold in the United States save one: In the case of financial products, the two parties no longer vigorously negotiate; consumers typically have little say on the terms of credit agreements—it's take it or leave it. The notion that the ordinary consumer is somehow on an equal footing with a $1 trillion megabank is absurd. The terms for credit cards, mortgages, and car loans are bloated, eye-straining treatises that even experienced lawyers have difficulty parsing. The past two decades have brought us universal default, double-cycle billing, teaser-rate mortgages, and negative amortization—concepts whose main function is to confuse and suck money from unsuspecting consumers.

Treating financial contracts like other products would change all that. The current jumble of federal and state regulations should be reconceived and enforced by a comprehensive new regulatory body, analogous to the CPSC. A Consumer Credit Safety Commission would make financial products more transparent, get rid of tricks and traps, and give consumers the tools to make prudent financial decisions.

Ultimately, safety regulations could help make the market for financial products as efficient as the market for physical products. Shorter contracts and clearer terms could replace lenders' current race to the bottom with a race to the top, based on consumer friendliness and fairness. Obviously, this would benefit consumers, by reducing loan defaults and foreclosure rates. Equally important, predictable payments and low default rates would benefit the economy and help avoid the kind of boom-and-bust financial cycle that has proved so devastating.

The moment is right to rethink our consumer credit laws. Growing U.S. consumption has supported the global economy, but the American family simply cannot carry that load any longer. Declining median incomes, combined with the rising costs of housing, health care, child care, transportation, and food, have left families in a deeper economic hole than ever before. They have turned to credit to finance basic necessities, but that is a short-term strategy, and time is running out. Today one in six mortgages is upside down, and 50 million families can't pay off their credit card bills. Last year one out of seven households was called by a debt collector. More than a million people declared bankruptcy. Foreclosure has reached levels unmatched since the Great Depression. This crisis highlights the urgent plight of the middle class, but the trend started decades ago.

America's advantages in innovation and productiveness are rooted in a vibrant middle class that still believes in the possibility of success. Its members can no longer afford tricky financial products, and the market can't afford them either—they destabilize families and the economy alike. Applying basic safety standards to this segment would provide badly needed security for consumers, investors, and the global economy.

ELIZABETH WARREN, the Leo Gottlieb Professor of Law at Harvard Law School in Cambridge, Massachusetts, has written eight books and more than 100 scholarly articles dealing with credit and economic stress. She is a member of the Congressional Oversight Panel for the $700 billion U.S. bailout.

AMELIA TYAGI, a former McKinsey consultant, is a cofounder and the COO of the Business Talent Group in Los Angeles. They are the coauthors of *The Two-Income Trap* (Basic Books, 2003) and *All Your Worth* (Free Press, 2005).

Now's the Time to Invest in Africa

> Past exhortations for businesses to invest in Africa have provoked skepticism or led to disappointing results. But new research shows that a number of sub-Saharan countries have achieved stability, adopted favorable policies and incentives, and now offer an inviting climate for investment and rates of return higher than those found in other developing countries.

By Paul Collier and Jean-Louis Warnholz

Over the years many misguided pronouncements have touted the improved economic prospects of Africa, home to a large proportion of the world's billion poorest people. The late 1990s even saw a slight economic resurgence, dubbed an "African renaissance," but it fizzled, and a gloomy view of the continent as too unstable for investment other than in mining and oil seemed to settle over corporate boardrooms.

But reliable data show that a number of sub-Saharan nations have emerged from conflict in stable condition and that new macroeconomic forces are poised to have a profound effect—despite the global economic downturn. For example, the International Monetary Fund's World Economic Outlook, released in October 2008, projected economic growth of 6.3% for sub-Saharan Africa in 2009, with Uganda, Tanzania, and Nigeria exceeding 8% growth. Our research on African companies indicates that the continent offers competitive manufacturing sites, IT outsourcing, and construction services. There is real opportunity on the ground in Africa.

Multinationals and investors should bear these developments in mind:

Stability The periods of catastrophic government action that slowed growth in past decades have become much less frequent. The failures in Ghana, Uganda, Tanzania, and Nigeria in the 1970s and 1980s were profound learning experiences for those countries, which have joined the list of today's success stories. Nigeria, for instance, has paid off its external debts, enacted prudent fiscal rules, and cleaned up its banking system.

Policy The more favorable policies of developed nations have laid the groundwork for growth: Many of Ghana's exports, for example, qualify for duty-free access to EU and U.S. markets. Policies within African countries have boosted local economies: Rwanda, for instance, has made information and communications technologies the cornerstone of a new growth strategy, setting up the ICT Park in Kigali, its capital.

Profits Our study of 2002–2007 financial data from all the Africa-based publicly traded companies for which data were available (a total of 954, mostly in manufacturing and services) shows that many of these firms are highly profitable. (For foreign-owned companies we looked only at the performance of the African entities.) In part because of low labor costs and gains in operational efficiency, the average annual return on capital of the companies studied was 65% to 70% higher than that of comparable firms in China, India, Indonesia, and Vietnam. The median profit margin was

11%—better than the comparable figures for Asia and South America. Our analysis of World Bank data on 1,869 African companies confirms these findings.

Opportunity Construction companies, call centers, and IT services are among the region's most successful businesses. The engineering services company Gasabo 3D Design, located in Kigali's ICT Park, uses computer technology to transform drawings into three-dimensional models for customers at a highly competitive hourly rate of US$10.

Years have passed since investors updated their view of Africa's promise. The time is ripe for multinationals to rethink sub-Saharan opportunities and simultaneously to help the region achieve its promise by contributing much-needed capital, business skills, and global connections.

PAUL COLLIER, author of *The Bottom Billion* (Oxford, 2007), is a professor of economics and the director of the Centre for the Study of African Economies at the University of Oxford in England.

JEAN-LOUIS WARNHOLZ is a researcher at the Centre for the Study of African Economies and a consultant on business development in emerging markets.

Just Because I'm Nice, Don't Assume I'm Dumb

> We often judge colleagues on the basis of their perceived warmth and competence, finding clues to these qualities in stereotypes rooted in race, gender, or nationality. Many of our decisions about fellow workers are thus premised on faulty data—harming judged and judgers alike.

By Amy J.C. Cuddy

When we encounter someone new, we quickly seek answers to two questions rooted in the evolutionary need to make correct survival decisions: What are this person's intentions toward me? and Is this person capable of acting on those intentions?

Because we lack the brainpower to weigh someone's true merits quickly, we seize on our sometimes mistaken answers to these questions and rate the person high or low on imaginary scales of intention and capability—or, to use simpler terminology, warmth and competence. Recent psychological research involving thousands of people from two dozen nations shows that this way of thinking is remarkably widespread. Moreover, a number of studies show that warmth and competence assessments determine whether and how we intend to interact with others: We like to assist people we view as warm and block those we see as cold; we desire to associate with people we consider competent and ignore those we consider incompetent.

Inevitably, of course, we find clues to warmth and competence in stereotypes based on people's race, gender, or nationality. Thus many of our decisions about whom to trust, doubt, defend, attack, hire, or fire are based on faulty data.

The warmth/competence model, which Susan Fiske, Peter Glick, and I have presented in more than a dozen academic articles over the past few years, illuminates a great deal of behavior—for example, why people disrespect the elderly while feeling positive toward them (elders are seen as incompetent but warm). Such attitudes weren't well explained by the prevailing psychological view of prejudice—namely, that people simply favor "us" and dislike "them."

Inaccurate warmth/competence judgments can lead managers to trust untrustworthy associates or undervalue potentially important connections with people. They can also undermine companies' efforts to build effective teams, identify lucrative opportunities, and retain good employees. For example, mothers, like the elderly, are chronically stereotyped as less competent (although warmer) than other workers and as a result are often underpromoted and underpaid.

Our and others' research has yielded another important finding: People tend to see warmth and competence as inversely related. If there's an apparent surplus of one trait, they infer a deficit of the other. ("She's so sweet. . . . She'd probably be inept in the boardroom.") So how can managers use the warmth/competence model to make better judgments? I recommend a two-part approach.

Don't take shortcuts. Virtually everyone uses stereotypes to make snap judgments. But when facing personnel decisions, managers should push themselves to be aware of how they form impressions. They should avoid sizing people up on the basis of stereotypical perceptions of warmth and competence.

Separate the two dimensions. It's not a zero-sum game: Warmth and competence aren't mutually exclusive. Managers should ask themselves, for example, whether that highly competent technician also has social or customer skills that could be useful to the company.

These simple reality checks can help managers see past social categories and recognize individuals' true talents, thus avoiding the high cost of mistaken judgments.

AMY J.C. CUDDY is an assistant professor at Harvard Business School in Boston.

Forget Citibank—
Borrow from Bob

> The financial crisis will trigger an increase in peer-to-peer financing. Already Lending Club and other organizations are demonstrating how novel approaches to credit scoring—including algorithms to analyze the reputations of social-network members—can reduce risk. As peer financing matures, traditional banking will converge with peer networks.

By John Sviokla

With consumer credit still tight, peer-to-peer lending is on the rise. Why? For one thing, human society naturally evolves to create pools of capital with which to fund ideas and absorb risk. Roman legionnaires insured one another by swearing to care for the families of comrades lost in battle. The creation of the shared stock corporation allowed for bigger and bigger risks to be taken. Whenever people come together to create a pool of capital, the potential for wealth creation blossoms.

For another, peer-to-peer lending is cheaper than consumer credit. Lending Club's rate for the best credit risks is 7.88%, whereas the bank rate for personal loans, on average, is over 13%. A credit-worthy borrower gets the money faster and for 5% less.

Why now? First, the internet and social networks enable peer-to-peer interaction on an unprecedented scale. Second, electronic mechanisms for assessing potential customers are emerging. Lending Club starts with traditional credit scoring and adds a proprietary assessment of customers' reputations within their social networks. You may think of Facebook as fun and games, but important underwriting information is hidden in there for those who know how to look.

So what? A profound secondary effect of the down market will be an increase in the availability of peer-to-peer finance and its convergence with traditional lending. My bet is that mainstream investors and banks will cherry-pick the best investors in Lending Club and other systems—reducing risk by tapping their superior credit-assessment capabilities—

and fund them to grant more and bigger loans. Moreover, within five years every major bank will probably have its own peer-to-peer lending network.

If innovative legislation were drafted to allow peer-to-peer risk coverage, similar transactions might begin to flourish in the insurance market. Precise knowledge of local conditions would allow individuals to band together in order to underwrite the cost of insuring properties in safe neighborhoods or to make insurance more widely available in higher-risk neighborhoods.

The current economic constraints will only accelerate the growth of these new entities. I predict that they will be among the most important financial-services innovations in the coming decade.

JOHN SVIOKLA is the vice chairman and director of innovation and research at Diamond Management and Technology Consultants in Chicago.

Harnessing Social Pressure

> Social pressure can be an effective tool for encouraging desired (or discouraging undesired) behavior in customers. For example, if you want hotel guests to reuse towels, let them know that most of a room's previous occupants did just that. But social pressure can cause unintended consequences: Utility customers commended for using less power than their neighbors upped consumption.

By Noah J. Goldstein

Marketers are good at using peer influence to sell products, but few executives understand that it can motivate customers to help companies achieve other goals, such as saving money. Even fewer seem to be aware that the improper use of peer influence can elicit behaviors contrary to what was intended.

Hotels, for example, don't exploit peer influence when trying to get guests to reuse towels, even though the daily cost of providing fresh ones can run to $1.50 a room. My colleagues and I set out to see if we could boost participation in one hotel's towel-reuse program by placing signs with various messages in randomly chosen rooms. We increased participation by 26% over the standard environmental appeal by truthfully stating that the majority of other hotel guests reused their towels. The increase in compliance was even greater when we communicated that most of the guests who had stayed in that particular room were reusers.

But peer influence can have strange effects. In a study led by the social psychologist Robert Cialdini, signs at Arizona's Petrified Forest National Park lamenting that many previous visitors had stolen petrified wood not only proved less effective at reducing pilferage than signs simply asking visitors not to take souvenirs, but resulted in more theft than when no signs at all were displayed. And in research I conducted with Wesley Schultz and several colleagues, California households that were informed they were using more electricity than their neighbors reduced their consumption, but those informed that they were using less increased their consumption by 8.6%.

The lesson is that people respond strongly to messages about the behavior of others, particularly similar others; the more similar the other people, the more potent the effect. But beware: A publicized behavioral norm becomes a "magnetic middle," drawing people toward it. To avoid inadvertently encouraging your best-behaved customers to backslide, try showing approval for their behavior. When the message to the below-norm California electricity users included a smiley face as a sign of approval, those households continued to consume at their original low rate.

NOAH J. GOLDSTEIN is an assistant professor at UCLA Anderson School of Management in Los Angeles and a coauthor of *Yes!: 50 Scientifically Proven Ways to Be Persuasive* (Free Press, 2008).

The Rise of Forensic Economics

> Specially trained economists can spot patterns or conditions that are likely to suggest or foster fraud and other forms of corruption. The author argues for the creation of a global forensic economics lab modeled on the international crime-fighting agency Interpol.

By Raymond Fisman

In August 2008 the Swiss police raided a number of offices of Alstom, a French company that had paid bribes to secure infrastructure contracts worldwide. The Alstom scandal—and corruption at companies such as Siemens and Halliburton—were uncovered by vigilant auditors and smart law-enforcement officials. These aren't the only people unearthing illicit transactions, however. Some economists have recently turned into detectives, pioneering the field of forensic economics.

Forensic economists don't investigate specific crimes or individual wrongdoing; they analyze the incentives underlying criminal activity and then use conventional tools to look for the footprints that wrongdoers' actions have left in the data. Which companies were shipping arms to Angola in violation of a UN embargo? Economists looked at stock market reactions to news of a ceasefire in Angola to see which stocks suffered the most: Presumably the embargo violators had the most to lose from an end to the fighting. What goods were smuggled into China from Hong Kong in the late 1990s? When I compared records of Hong Kong's exports with those of China's imports, I found that high-tariff goods were most likely to "disappear" in transit. Other forensic economists have uncovered evidence of options backdating, payola in the UN oil-for-food program, and vote trading among figure-skating judges at the Winter Olympics.

Forensic economists could have uncovered such problems sooner if they had been able to access data that only governments possess. That's why we should create a global forensic economics laboratory to coordinate the work of government authorities and researchers, so that together they can better fight corruption. Had I been able to work with China's customs agencies, I could have found smuggling patterns today rather than having to look back at the 1990s. If forensic economists are to detect the sort of bribery Alstom engaged in, they will need better data on cross-border financial flows than are in the public domain. And if governments gave them access, they would have more useful and interesting problems to study, and their results would be more relevant to current policy. They still wouldn't be able to dig up evidence of crimes by specific companies, but the patterns they uncovered would help focus enforcement efforts on the sectors or countries with the most suspicious activity.

Collaboration can be a two-way street. Economists could draw on the experience of in-the-trenches bureaucrats and police officers to find promising leads. Rather than make do with off-the-shelf data, they could design research programs around governments' anticorruption efforts, and if governments were willing to experiment with those efforts, economists could follow up with audits to examine their impact. Happily, collaboration between academe and government is well established, as is global cooperation to combat criminal activity: For nearly 100 years Interpol has coordinated efforts to fight transnational crime.

Crunching numbers won't generate the same excitement that other methods of fighting crime do; we economists will never appear on the evening news busting down doors with guns blazing. But data could be a critical weapon in the anticorruption arsenal if governments gave forensic economists the opportunity to put them to good use.

RAYMOND FISMAN is the Lambert Family Professor of Social Enterprise at Columbia Business School in New York. He is a coauthor, with Edward Miguel, of *Economic Gangsters* (Princeton, 2008).

A Looming American Diaspora

> The U.S. monopoly on leading-edge opportunities is at an end. The world's best and brightest no longer look exclusively to America, and even top U.S. talent is beginning to look elsewhere.

By Paul Saffo

While U.S. companies are worrying about how to recruit talent from abroad in the face of increasingly stringent immigration rules, a different and far more significant challenge is quietly building. When young knowledge workers look for a job today, they seriously consider companies half a world away. Homegrown American talent is moving abroad, in what could become a huge shift in the world economic order.

Early warning signs abound. Look at Singapore's success in recruiting top U.S. academics to its universities and research centers: It lured the world's leading seismologist away from Cal Tech and the number two scientist at the National Institutes of Health away from that organization. Silicon Valley expatriates have been moving to China in a small but steady stream. Farmers from the Midwest are using their high-tech methods to make a new start in Brazil, where real estate is cheap.

The United States' current economic woes are accelerating this trend. The trickle that has started at the top will become a flood as mid-career executives look for new opportunities abroad. Of course, even the best manager will struggle if he or she doesn't speak the local language. But one can get by in India with English only, and Spanish is relatively easy to learn. Moreover, when the children of today's expats enter the workforce, they'll reap a huge advantage from knowing the second language—Chinese, Portuguese, Hindustani—they learned to speak at home as youngsters. More and more parents are discovering that a multilingual education can help in guaranteeing lifelong employability for their offspring.

Government policy will be crucial in determining how well U.S. companies respond to the increasing diaspora of American talent. Lawmakers must not resort to knowledge protectionism—for instance, by requiring people who attend state-funded universities to spend a certain amount of their working life in the United States. Rather, they must ensure that America remains the most congenial place for high-tech enterprises and continues to attract foreign students to its universities and foreign workers to its companies.

The U.S. monopoly on leading-edge opportunities is at an end. The world's best and brightest no longer assume that their future lies exclusively in the United States, and America's best are coming to agree: Their path to a dream career may well lead them overseas.

PAUL SAFFO is a technology forecaster based in Silicon Valley.

Institutional Memory Goes Digital

> Suppose all your company meetings could be faithfully captured in searchable, high-quality digital video, including every word, gesture, yawn, and rolling of the eyes. How might that be both a blessing and a curse? This isn't an idle question—the technology needed to develop such systems is within reach.

By Gurdeep Singh Pall and Rita Gunther McGrath

Suppose every utterance and facial expression at a meeting were routinely captured and archived in high-definition digital video recordings—searchable and available in perpetuity. Would this be a godsend or a nightmare? The answer is probably both, but we're about to find out for sure. Within a few years, a synthesis of technologies from an array of companies will make possible a "total recall system," or TRS, that can produce such recordings.

Let's say you miss an important meeting. Instead of having to piece it together from the contradictory accounts of those who were there, you will be able to log in to your company's TRS and search a recording of the meeting for the stuff you really care about. Or maybe you'd like to revisit discussions that stretched over a series of meetings and led to an important decision for which you are partly accountable. All the deliberations along the way—advocacy, misgivings, evolving positions—are there for your review. Of course, if the decision turns out to have been a bad one, the record will likewise be there to vindicate or implicate dissenters and promoters alike.

Indeed, TRS is a double-edged sword. A silly suggestion made in a brainstorming meeting might end up on YouTube, Yahoo Video, or MSN Video. Every thoughtless or sarcastic comment could potentially come back to haunt its maker in an HR inquiry or a lawsuit. Recorded content would be discoverable, potentially increasing the already staggering costs and complexity of litigation. Clearly, digital-rights protections that prevent the unauthorized from accessing these records will be hugely important.

On the other hand, companies could use the recordings to defend themselves in court. And software programs will be able to dig through the recordings to identify people's expertise and network ties, making it possible to find everyone who has mentioned a subject of interest, on what occasion, and to whom.

The next frontier is technology that can recognize faces and interpret gestures and expressions. (Does John Doe always twitch when he makes commitments he doesn't keep?) These capabilities should be available in a decade. Yes, Big Brother may ultimately capture everything we say and do at a meeting, with consequences both good and bad.

GURDEEP SINGH PALL is the corporate vice president of Microsoft's Unified Communications Group, in Redmond, Washington.

RITA GUNTHER MCGRATH is an associate professor of management at Columbia Business School in New York.

The Business of Biomimicry

> Profitable businesses can be built around innovations copied from nature, a discipline known as biomimicry. Advanced solar-cell technology, for example, demonstrates that materials modeled on plant photosynthesis can offer both improved economics and performance advantages over traditional solar cells—with fewer environmental consequences.

By Janine M. Benyus and Gunter A.M. Pauli

Biomimics draw inspiration for new product designs from biological processes, physical traits, and behavioral strategies observed in nature. The classic example of biomimicry innovation is Velcro, whose inventor, George de Mestral, observed that the hooked tips of thistle seeds caused them to stick to the fur of his dog. Today we look ever more systematically to nature for sustainable solutions to a host of practical problems—for which existing solutions are often environmentally unfriendly or energy inefficient. We believe that now is an opportune time for global businesses to develop profitably around some of the ideas nature offers. One innovation—dye-sensitized solar cells (DSSCs)—presents an intriguing example.

The DSSC Advantage

DSSC materials can collect light at shallow angles, capture dim as well as full sun, and work in scorching temperatures (all of which bedevil traditional photovoltaics). They can go where silicon panels can't: on vertical surfaces, in the shaded lower "canopy" of cities, in the sunless cores of buildings, and in desert or tropical locations. In the evolution of solar cells, they are the equivalent of aquatic life's learning to live on land, opening a vast array of new habitats.

The Biological Model

What was needed was something as self-reliant and elegantly capable as a leaf. Emulation of plant photosynthesis led to the development of dye-sensitized solar cells.

Sunlight energy

Electrolyte

Glass pane (electrode)

Titanium dioxide

Ruthenium dye

Device to be powered

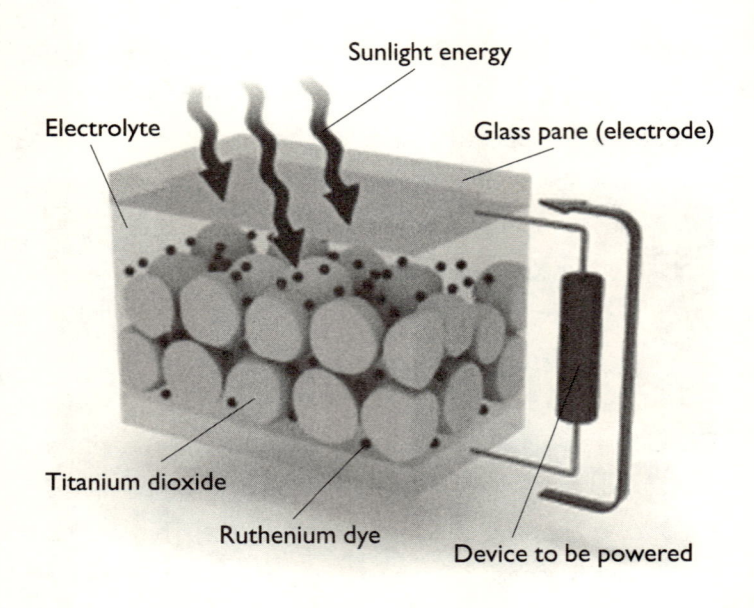

The scientists Michael Grätzel and Brian O'Regan combined between two panes of glass ruthenium-polypyridine dye (equivalent to the leaf pigment chlorophyll), whose electrons are activated by sunlight; titanium dioxide, a transmission medium that shuttles activated ruthenium electrons to a conductive electrode, through the device to be powered, and back through a second electrode to complete a circuit; and an electrolytic liquid that recharges the ruthenium for another round of activation.

Expanding the Solar-Cell Market

Although DSSCs are currently less efficient than traditional photovoltaic cells, they're 60% cheaper to produce and more versatile—they can be made into flexible films or fibers in a process similar to ink-jet printing. Two companies—Konarka, of Lowell, Massachusetts, and Dyesol, of New South Wales, Australia—stand out for having pioneered advances in DSSC materials and manufacturing technologies that lower costs and improve performance.

One Promising Solution. Inexpensive, nontoxic solar harvesters can work not only on roofs but also on vertical, curved, shaded, or even indoor surfaces. Millions of distributed harvesters could be networked on a neighborhood scale or used alone when power grids failed. Steelmakers are already testing ways of incorporating DSSCs into structural steel. Imagine the Golden Gate Bridge doubling as a power plant.

Assault on Batteries. At present, DSSCs can't claim to compete with the traditional grid. But as a power source for small appliances, toys, flashlights, and other devices, the technology is an economical alternative to batteries—which are 100 times as expensive per kilowatt hour as power from the grid and become highly polluting once discarded.

JANINE M. BENYUS is president of the board of the Biomimicry Institute in Missoula, Montana, and the author of *Biomimicry: Innovation Inspired by Nature* (William Morrow, 1997). **GUNTER A.M. PAULI** is the author of 17 books and the founding director of ZERI (Zero Emissions Research and Initiatives), a global network of science and business innovators.

The IKEA Effect: When Labor Leads to Love

> People place a disproportionately high value on products they had a hand in making. They'd rather buy their own amateurish origami than something made by a pro. The IKEA effect may explain why business managers keep failing projects alive: because of all the time and effort they've invested.

By Michael I. Norton

Labor is not just a meaningful experience—it's also a marketable one. When instant cake mixes were introduced, in the 1950s, housewives were initially resistant: The mixes were too easy, suggesting that their labor was undervalued. When manufacturers changed the recipe to require the addition of an egg, adoption rose dramatically. Ironically, increasing the labor involved—making the task more arduous—led to greater liking.

Research conducted with my colleagues Daniel Mochon, of Yale University, and Dan Ariely, of Duke University, shows that labor enhances affection for its results. When people construct products themselves, from bookshelves to Build-a-Bears, they come to overvalue their (often poorly made) creations. We call this phenomenon the IKEA effect, in honor of the wildly successful Swedish manufacturer whose products typically arrive with some assembly required.

In one of our studies we asked people to fold origami and then to bid on their own creations along with other people's. They were consistently willing to pay more for their own origami. In fact, they were so enamored of their amateurish creations that they valued them as highly as origami made by experts.

We also investigated the limits of the IKEA effect, showing that labor leads to higher valuation only when the labor is fruitful: When participants failed to complete an effortful task, the IKEA effect dissipated. Our research suggests that consumers may be willing to pay a premium for do-it-yourself projects, but there's an important caveat: Companies hoping to persuade their customers to assume labor costs—for example, by nudging them toward self-service through internet channels—should be careful to create tasks difficult enough to lead to higher valuation but not so difficult that customers can't complete them.

Finally, the IKEA effect has broader implications for organizational dynamics: It contributes to the sunk cost effect, whereby managers continue to devote resources to (sometimes failing) projects in which they have invested their labor, and to the not-invented-here syndrome, whereby they discount good ideas developed elsewhere in favor of their (sometimes inferior) internally developed ideas. Managers should keep in mind that ideas they have come to love because they invested their own labor in them may not be as highly valued by their coworkers—or their customers.

MICHAEL I. NORTON is an assistant professor at Harvard Business School in Boston.

Beware Global Cooling

> Data can be deceptive when interpreted improperly.
> Intervals of falling temperatures, lasting from several
> years to decades, may tempt societies to diminish
> efforts aimed at reducing greenhouse gases—but the
> long-term trend is unmistakable.
>
> **By Peter Schwartz**

If the global temperature trends of the past several decades continue, and if recent climate modeling is right, the earth will probably cool over the next few years. Some will surely take a string of cooler years as a signal that the experts got it wrong: The earth isn't warming after all, and we can stop fretting about greenhouse-gas emissions.

In the mid-1970s I was part of a U.S. Energy Research and Development Administration team commissioned to determine whether recent climatic cooling indicated that the earth was entering a "little ice age" like the one that depressed global temperatures between the fourteenth and the late nineteenth centuries. In time the answer became clear: The cooling that had begun in the 1960s was a mere blip in a long-term warming trend.

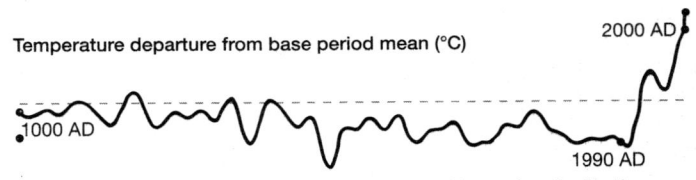

Temperature departure from base period mean (°C)

[Graph showing temperature from 1000 AD to 2000 AD, with a sharp rise near 1990 AD]

The long-term trend is striking: After a century of rapid warming, the Northern Hemisphere is hotter than it's been in a thousand years.

Source: M. E. Mann

Today we may be experiencing another such cooling blip. Last spring the climate scientist Noel Keenlyside and colleagues published a provocative paper in *Nature* forecasting a decade of slight global cooling—particularly over the North Atlantic, North America, and Western Europe—as natural climate variations offset projected man-made warming.

Indeed, the earth is slightly cooler today than it was in 2005—but its average temperature is increasing from one decade to the next. An annual wobble occurs around that rising mean. Consider temperature trends over the past 35 years: A relatively warm year has typically been followed by a string of cooler years. If this pattern holds, temperatures may well remain below their 2005 peak for several more years. But this short-term pattern masks the longer-term trend: The earth's temperature is climbing abruptly. Misreading our current cooling blip as a turning point—and throttling back on greenhouse-gas reductions—would be a dangerous mistake.

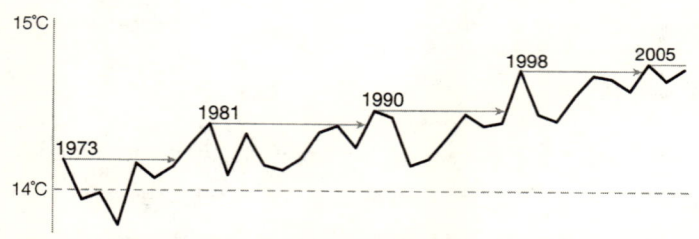

Average global temperature may dip periodically, but the recent trend is clear: Each hot year is followed after a lag by an even hotter one.

Source: Goddard Institute for Space Studies

PETER SCHWARTZ is a cofounder and the chairman of Global Business Network, a Monitor Group company, in San Francisco.

The Dynamics of Personal Influence

> New research shows that personal influence is a relatively short-range phenomenon, dissipating entirely at three degrees of remove from the person who exercises it. This has implications for business, where the success of campaigns to foster, say, creativity or worker safety may hinge on enlisting employees to influence colleagues' behavior.

By Nicholas A. Christakis

You may have noticed how fashions in clothes or music spread through social networks. It turns out that all kinds of conditions and behaviors—including obesity, smoking, altruism, voting, and happiness—can flow through them as well. Yet although a person may be connected to other people by six degrees of separation, he or she is influenced only by those up to three degrees away. My colleague James Fowler and I have also found that a person's influence progressively diminishes as the degrees of separation increase. For example, the risk for smoking in a person connected to a smoker (that is, at one degree of separation) is 61% higher, on average, than would be expected as a result of chance. It is 29% higher if the friends of that person's friends smoke, and 11% higher if the friends of the person's friends' friends smoke. By the fourth degree of separation there is no longer an increase in risk. To take another example, we have found that a person is 15% likelier to be happy if his or her friends are happy, 10% likelier if the friends' friends are happy, and 6% likelier if the friends of those friends' friends are happy.

What does all this mean for businesses? Pharmaceutical companies might target physicians more efficiently by exploiting their tendency to be influenced by other physicians to whom they are connected. Workplace-safety initiatives might benefit from the understanding that one person who adopts safer practices influences others to do so. Efforts to foster creativity or innovation might depend on the degree of separation of the relevant parties. And groups of customers—including customers who have online connections—might be strategically targeted so as to take advantage of their influence on one another.

NICHOLAS A. CHRISTAKIS is a physician and a professor of sociology at Harvard University in Cambridge, Massachusetts.

Western Union World

> Immigrants are an important customer pool that most businesses neglect. Not only do they buy products for their own use, but they influence and economically support families and friends in their countries of origin. They are untapped brand emissaries reaching a global network of unseen consumers.

By Marcelo Suarez-Orozco

In a recession, where can you go to find an untapped and eager customer base? Look to the approximately 200 million migrants worldwide and their relatives back home—a pool of about half a billion potential customers. In 2007 expatriates remitted some $350 billion—more than three times what the wealthy member states of the Organisation for Economic Co-operation and Development gave in aid to the entire developing world—to relatives left behind. In the United

States the purchasing power of Latinos, by far the largest immigrant group, is now well over $800 billion.

Immigrants who send money and products home are powerful agents of influence in their own lands. One company that understands this is Western Union, which has more than doubled the number of its agent locations around the planet, to about 335,000 in some 200 countries and territories. In the five years from 2002 to 2007 the company's revenues grew from $2.7 billion to $4.9 billion. President and CEO Christina Gold told the *New York Times,* "Global migration is the cornerstone of how we've grown."

What do businesses need to know to serve the migrant millions?

First, the ability to bridge the old and the new is key to immigrants' self-image, adaptation, and success. Immigrants often rely on a dual frame of reference when making purchasing decisions: As they adapt to a new environment, they invariably combine brand loyalty with the cultural practices of their home countries. The newly arrived Mexican family will buy the mother a washing machine at Sears for Mother's Day, because that was the tradition in Mexico. To celebrate his son's acceptance to a good college, a Chinese father in San Francisco will take his high schooler to

McDonald's (rather than a high-end restaurant), because that is where he went in China after exam day. As these immigrants begin to adopt American cultural practices, opportunities will arise for companies attuned to the process of change.

Second, judging from their new consumption and lifestyle choices, immigrants are often more concerned with the image they project back home—where they are seen as trendsetters—than with the one they project in the new country. Witness the mansions built in Ghana by native-son doctors working in New York: Although these houses often remain empty, they are greatly admired by friends and relatives.

Third, immigrants tend to know much more about their new country than the new country knows about them. They're not even on the radar screens of many marketers in their adopted lands. Businesses that follow Western Union's example in understanding and engaging new arrivals will have an edge.

MARCELO SUAREZ-OROZCO is the Courtney Sale Ross University Professor of Globalization and Education at New York University.

State Capitalism Makes a Comeback

> Governments recently intervened forcefully in the banking and auto industries, echoing a trend with potentially greater long-term impact: the global resurgence of state-controlled enterprises. We chart the growing influence of state capitalism in four industry sectors.

By Ian Bremmer and Juan Pujadas

Recent and unprecedented government intervention in the banking and auto industries echoes a trend with potentially greater long-term impact: the reemergence of state-controlled enterprises around the world.

Not long ago, direct government management of business seemed an anachronism. The Marxist bureaucracies of the Soviet Union and its satellites had buckled under the burden of an unsustainable economic system. China, the world's remaining communist giant, was moving toward ever freer markets. Vestigial state-owned businesses in Western nations were being privatized, and the dynamism of Western economies—fueled by private wealth, private investment, and private enterprise—seemed to have permanently validated the liberal economic model. Some predicted the end of Westphalian sovereignty, as stateless corporate entities increasingly influenced world affairs.

But public wealth, public investment, and public enterprise have returned with a vengeance. We are entering an era in which governments again manage large entities and direct huge flows of capital. In numerous industries, emerging nations, led by China and Russia, are moving not to regulate markets but to command them.

Although the economic crisis has taken its toll on many state-owned enterprises, as it has on their private-sector counterparts, serious implications for free markets and international politics remain. For example, state-owned enterprises have been willing to forge alliances with other, often unstable governments, thus increasing risk across entire sectors through the creation of uncertain supply chains. The (often authoritarian) governments that are profiting from these enterprises will be tempted to take foreign-policy gambles, confident that their market clout in critical sectors will limit the response of concerned countries. In developed economies, the fear that state-owned enterprises are driven primarily by politics is already resulting in regulatory hurdles that could hinder economic growth.

Government-affiliated entities now have a leading position or growing influence in a number of sectors.

Asset Management

The rise of sovereign wealth funds—12 new ones have been established since 2005, only some of them based on oil wealth—reflect governments' growing ownership role in private enterprise.

Abu Dhabi Investment Authority (UAE)
Government Pension Fund–Global (Norway)
Saudi Arabian Monetary Authority
Government of Singapore Investment Corporation
Kuwait Investment Authority
China Investment Corporation
Hong Kong Exchange Fund
Temasek (Singapore)
Reserve and National Wealth funds (Russia)
The Blackstone Group (U.S.)
The Carlyle Group (U.S.)
Bain Capital (U.S.)
Queensland Investment Corporation (Australia)
Kohlberg Kravis Roberts (U.S.)
TPG (U.S.)

Wholly or partly state-owned enterprises
Private sector companies

Assets under management (as of June 2008)   US$800B

Shipping

Two state-owned Chinese shipping companies are among the largest worldwide, as measured by the capacity of their operating fleets.

A. P. Moller–Maersk (Denmark)	
Mediterranean Shipping (Switzerland)	
CMA CGM Group (France)	
Evergreen Line (Taiwan, Hong Kong, UK, Italy)	
Hapag-Lloyd (Germany)	
COSCO Container Lines Americas (China)	
APL (Singapore)	
CSCL (China)	
NYK (Japan)	
MOL (Japan)	

2.5 M

■ Wholly or partly state-owned enterprises
□ Private sector companies

TEU: 20-foot equivalent units (as of September 2008)

Energy

State-owned enterprises dominate a ranking of the top oil and gas companies that takes into account oil and natural gas reserves and production, refinery capacity, and sales volumes.

- Saudi Aramco (Saudi Arabia)
- NIOC (Iran)
- Exxon Mobil (U.S.)
- BP (UK)
- PDV (Venezuela)
- Royal Dutch Shell (UK, Netherlands)
- CNPC (China)
- ConocoPhillips (U.S.)
- Chevron (U.S.)
- Total (France)
- Pemex (Mexico)
- Gazprom (Russia)
- Sonatrach (Algeria)
- KPC (Kuwait)
- Petrobras (Brazil)

■ Wholly or partly state-owned enterprises
□ Private sector companies

PIW 2007 index (lower number = higher ranking) 120

Telecommunications

One company partly owned by the Chinese government has a market capitalization that represents close to 40% of the value of the top 10 firms in the global mobile telecom sector.

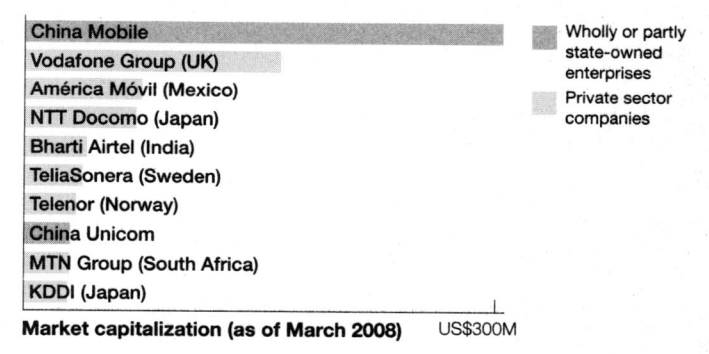

China Mobile	Wholly or partly state-owned enterprises
Vodafone Group (UK)	
América Móvil (Mexico)	Private sector companies
NTT Docomo (Japan)	
Bharti Airtel (India)	
TeliaSonera (Sweden)	
Telenor (Norway)	
China Unicom	
MTN Group (South Africa)	
KDDI (Japan)	

Market capitalization (as of March 2008) US$300M

Sources: **Asset Management:** J.P. Morgan; individual company data; Eurasia Group analysis **Shipping:** ASX-Alphaliner; Eurasia Group analysis **Energy:** Petroleum Intelligence Weekly **Telecommunications:** *Financial Times*; Eurasia Group analysis

---

IAN BREMMER is the president of Eurasia Group, a global political risk consultancy headquartered in New York, and a coauthor, with Preston Keat, of *The Fat Tail: The Power of Political Knowledge for Strategic Investing* (Oxford, 2009).

JUAN PUJADAS is the global and U.S. managing partner for advisory services at Price-waterhouseCoopers, based in New York.

Launching a Better Brain

> You may not know it yet, but one of your purposes in life should be to stimulate neuroplasticity—the creation of new brain cells. One way to do this is by shooting off rockets in the desert. But there are others.

By Steve Jurvetson

Our education systems and workplaces plunge us into deep mental ruts. They reward competencies that are self-reinforcing, not diversifying, and they encourage people to acquire domain expertise rather than to ask stupid questions and learn new things. We need to find our way out of these ruts and rekindle the creativity that many of us left behind in childhood.

As a kid, I loved playing with Legos. Now I build and launch model rockets. (In 2003, when I was browsing the local hobby shop for something fun to do with my son, I saw some rocket kits on the wall. My childhood was rediscovered!) Besides being flat-out fun, rocketry helps preserve my childlike mind, which continually learns and grows through play and discovery.

Human cognitive development peaks in the teen years, plateaus into our late thirties, and then begins a gradual descent that lasts until death. Rarely can people orchestrate their lives to provide regular mental pursuits capable of combating that decline.

The common wisdom is that after childhood we have a fixed number of neurons, which gradually die off during our lives, and that these neurons are organized in a fixed architecture. Not true: New neurons are born throughout life, and synaptic connections are being formed and erased all the time. This phenomenon is called neuroplasticity. Cognitive exercise—or the lack of it—can dial the rate of rewiring up or down.

This explains, in part, why—besides having fun—I would want to shoot off rockets in the desert. To be sure, my business life is engaging and demanding. But its rhythms are familiar and often predictable. So I've learned to seek out unaccustomed inputs. I keep challenging my mind by mastering new skills. (Last year I learned how to fiberglass and how to take a rocket supersonic.)

My work, which involves evaluating start-up businesses and their leaders, benefits from this. I am comfortable in the midst of new ideas and approaches, from nanotechnology to synthetic biology. And I'm not an odd man out in this regard—my firm's experience shows that a playful culture bears fruit.

Rocketry may not be for everyone. But I can't imagine a single business leader who wouldn't benefit from engaging in some pursuit—novel writing, wood carving, Civil War reenactment, whatever—that transcends the routine world and challenges the brain. Cognitive exercise will keep you agile, adaptive, and fit for life, in business and beyond.

And if you'd like to try rocketry, let me know, at stevej@boxbe.com.

STEVE JURVETSON is a managing director of the venture capital firm Draper Fisher Jurvetson in Menlo Park, California.

Stumbling to a Longer Life

> Arakawa and Madeline Gins—architects who have declared their "intention not to die"—create uncomfortably destabilizing spaces designed to enhance longevity. Steeply undulating concrete floors festooned with cobblelike protrusions express their belief that environments should require occupants to be conscious of how they move. Ultimately, the architects say, such conditions keep an excess of comfort from degrading physical skills.

By Lew McCreary

Next time your company reconfigures an interior space or builds itself a new headquarters, consider how the design you select might help employees live longer.

The architects Arakawa (who goes by his last name only) and Madeline Gins, his wife and longtime collaborator, have declared their "intention not to die." To that end (or not, as the case may be), they've created architectural features that promote "death resistance" by requiring people to navigate unsettling, disorienting, and dangerous but whimsical spaces.

Their eccentrically designed Bioscleave House, in East Hampton, New York—the subject of a sometimes incredulous April 2008 *New York Times* article by the architecture writer Fred A. Bernstein—features interior elements of topography, texture, color, and light that, taken together, are meant to extend the residents' life spans. As Bernstein wrote in the *Times*, "Its architecture makes people use their bodies in unexpected ways to maintain equilibrium, and that, [Gins] said, will stimulate their immune systems."

On their website (www.reversibledestiny.org) the pair say they have spent the better part of four decades "studying how architecture might best be used to sustain life." In the conventional sense, of course, architecture is the design of shelter, and shelter protects us from inhospitable elements. But Arakawa and Gins mean to accomplish something else: to design shelters whose discombobulating layouts, uneven surfaces, and jarring colors safeguard motor, visual, and cognitive skills from the degenerative effects of too much ease and creature comfort.

They have created residential lofts in Mitaka, Japan, that, in the dreamy language of their website, require occupants to "examine minutely the actions they take and ... recalibrate their equanimity and self-possession, causing them to doubt themselves long enough to find a way to reinvent themselves."

In other words, they design space that forces people to think carefully about where and how they move through it—at the very least, an interesting way of curing tedium and promoting alertness.

LEW MCCREARY is a senior editor at HBR.

What You Need to Know About the Semantic Web

> Sooner rather than later, a quiet technology revolution will radically change the way the internet works—organizing and presenting web content not as documents but as items of data interlinked on the basis of what they mean and how they are related. There are gnarly implications for existing search technologies and for businesses with a significant online presence.

By Tom Ilube

A quiet technology revolution—one that will radically change the way the internet works—is likely to catch much of the world off guard. It involves the "semantic web"—a way of organizing and presenting web content not as documents but as items of data that are linked by both meaning and relationship. A shockingly high percentage of businesspeople have never even heard of the semantic web, which bodes ill for their ability to position their organizations to cope with its implications or exploit its opportunities.

The semantic web was envisioned nearly 15 years ago by Sir Tim Berners-Lee, inventor of the World Wide Web, and is being developed within the World Wide Web Consortium (W3C), which Berners-Lee directs. Indeed, some 23 billion data relationships have been coded since 2000 (more than half of them in the past year alone) using a protocol known as Resource Description Framework (RDF).

The pieces of data that make up a present-day HTML-based document are not, for lack of a better term, aware of their relationships with the document's other pieces of data (or data in other documents). The semantic web, however, is built on standards and protocols that clearly define the relationship of each data item to others—not just within the document but wherever those other data may be on the entire web. At present, people must wade through and make sense of search results. The semantic web would enable computers to interact with other computers to assemble data items that are precisely responsive to highly specific queries.

Suppose you're interested in Shakespeare's many references to adultery. Whereas a conventional search would return thousands of separate documents, which you would then have to ransack for the exact material you want, a semantic web query would extract data from those thousands of documents and assemble a single, convenient collection of all the relevant references.

This means, among other things, that today's search engines (and the business models they sustain) would have to be retooled or replaced in order to work in a semantic web. In the retooled world, users could easily replicate the full functionality and flexibility of Facebook, MySpace, or LinkedIn using an open, standards-based RDF approach. Thus the semantic web would cut out the intermediary and restore control of personal information to the individuals who are its true owners.

Online retailers, music stores, travel agents, game sites, media publishers, and myriad others need to absorb the implications of living in a rapidly emerging world of open, linked data. Business leaders must first understand what is going on and make sure that someone in their organization is immersed in semantic web issues and considering their implications. If you ask your CTO about the semantic web and he or she looks at you blankly, you've got a problem. Your technology team will have to devise an architectural road map for the semantic web over the next three to five years and to undertake the difficult work of transition.

Perhaps most important, try to see the semantic web from your customers' perspective. They won't care what it's called, only what it does. The enhanced customer experience resulting from services that draw on a global web of highly relevant data will render obsolete many websites that are considered today's best in class.

TOM ILUBE is a cofounder and the CEO of Garlik, a UK-based online-identity management service. He was named a World Economic Forum Technology Pioneer for 2008.

How Social Networks Network Best

> Within companies' social networks the combination of two distinct models—one for discovering information and one for integrating it—is shown to produce superior decisions and greater group productivity. Researchers used "sociometers" to monitor individuals' interactions.

By Alex Pentland

The humble bee has much to teach us about the flow of information in our own organizations. Bees, like human beings, are social animals, and evolution has provided them with elegant approaches to group decision making.

One of the most important group decisions made by a bee colony is where to locate the hive. Bees use a kind of "idea market" to guide their discovery: The colony sends out a small number of scouts to survey the environment. Returning scouts that have found promising sites signal their discoveries with a vigorous dance, thus recruiting more scouts to the better sites. The cycle of exploration and signaling continues until so many scouts are signaling in favor of the best site that a tipping point is reached.

The bees' decision making highlights both information discovery and information integration, two processes that are crucial to every organization but that have different requirements. A centralized structure works well for discovery, because the individual's role is to find information and report it back. In contrast, a richly connected network works best for integration and decision making, because it allows the individual to hear everyone else's opinion about the expected return from each of the alternatives. The bees' process suggests that organizations that alternate as needed between the centralized structure and the richly connected network can shape information flow to optimize both discovery and integration.

Recent studies at MIT reveal that this sort of oscillation may be characteristic of creative teams. One intriguing study tracked employees in the marketing division of a German bank by having them wear small sensors called sociometers for one month. Sociometers record data about face-to-face interactions such as participants' identities and the location and duration of the interaction. Analysis of the data showed that teams charged with creating new marketing campaigns oscillated between the centralized communication associated with discovery and densely interconnected conversations that were mostly with other team members. In contrast, the members of implementation groups showed little oscillation, speaking almost exclusively to other team members.

A second study demonstrated not only that creative teams had especially nimble social-communication networks, but also that the amount of oscillation correlated with how productive the creative group judged itself to be. In this study almost 40% of the variation in creative productivity could be attributed to an oscillating pattern of communication strategies for discovery and integration.

Delving deeper into the communication networks of several organizations illuminated the links between productivity and information flow even more. A recent MIT study found that in one organization the employees with the most extensive personal digital networks were 7% more productive than their colleagues—so Wikis and Web 2.0

tools may indeed improve productivity. In the same organization, however, the employees with the most cohesive face-to-face networks were 30% more productive. Electronic tools may well be suited to information discovery, but face-to-face communication, an oft-neglected part of the management process, best supports information integration—as bees already know.

ALEX PENTLAND is the Toshiba Professor of Media Arts and Sciences at MIT and director of human dynamics research at the MIT Media Lab in Cambridge, Massachusetts. He is the author of *Honest Signals: How They Shape Our World* (MIT, 2008), from which this article is drawn.

Should You Outsource Your Brain?

> Offshore outsourcers have a new and intriguing service offering: decision making. Providers—primarily in India—have developed sophisticated analytic tools, and clients are beginning to trust them with a variety of complicated business problems. Would you?

By Thomas H. Davenport and Bala Iyer

It wasn't easy, but over the past two decades business embraced the offshore outsourcing of various functions, including laborious back-office tasks, call-center activities, and routine business processes. Now a more cerebral function—decision making—is being added to the offshore services menu, as third-party providers structure decision alternatives, analyze data, and recommend or even take courses of action.

Are businesses really ready to outsource their thinking? The answer may depend on how much confidence-building experience they have had with analytics generally, since third-party decision making is an analytics-intensive undertaking.

The trend began quietly in the mid-1990s, at General Electric's captive offshore center in India. Though the center was set up to do back-office work, managers realized that employees there could also help with decision algorithms. Soon the operation had become the primary provider of decision tools for credit and risk analysis. When GE sold a stake in its offshore unit in 2004, the resulting company, Genpact, began to take on decision analysis for other clients.

Today several other offshore firms—Mu Sigma, MarketRX (acquired by Cognizant in 2007), and Inductis—also specialize in decision analysis; their clients include some of the largest U.S.-based firms. They're helping a major retailer to decide where to build new stores, a large auto insurance company to set rates for different customer subsets, a pharmaceutical giant to decide how to deploy its salespeople, and a leading office products retailer to decide which promotions and products to offer to which customers. Even large offshore vendors that previously specialized in IT, such as Cognizant, TCS, and Infosys, are beginning to develop an expertise in decision making.

Companies that outsource decision making report improvements in their decision processes and results. But how did they get comfortable with the idea of turning important business decisions over to third parties? Some say that the project structure was critical. The office products retailer, for example, recommends "4-1-1": four offshore analytics consultants, one consultant at the client site, and one well-connected client employee on the team. The onshore consultant is responsible for communication and coordination between the offshore team and the client. The employee's job is to ensure that the analysis is consistent with the decisions the organization wants to make, and to communicate the outcome to the appropriate executives. The result of a decision analysis is useful only if it's implemented, and offshore analysts can't easily influence executives to adopt a recommended action. It's also important that consultants on the vendor's team have deep domain expertise.

With a shortage of analytic skills in the United States and Western Europe and a ready supply in India, Eastern

Europe, and China, it's perhaps not surprising that organizations are now outsourcing these more cerebral functions.

THOMAS H. DAVENPORT is the President's Distinguished Professor of Information Technology and Management, and **BALA IYER** is an associate professor of information technology management, at Babson College in Wellesley, Massachusetts.

A Central Nervous System for the Earth

Great progress has been made in the design and production of low-cost, highly capable nanoscale sensors—the first step toward creating a global sensing network capable of monitoring every corner of Earth's natural and built environments. Researchers at Hewlett-Packard Labs are beginning to build the necessary infrastructure, and they're looking for businesses interested in joining pilot projects.

By R. Stanley Williams

Researchers are fast overcoming physical barriers to developing nanoscale materials and technologies. We can now create arrays of nanotechnology-based sensors capable of gathering data on virtually anything that can be measured. The rapidly falling cost and rising capability of these sensors hold the promise of an affordable planetwide sensing network. Such an infrastructure could monitor natural and built environments to provide situational awareness for urgent real-time interventions and global awareness for ongoing maintenance.

Potential applications include:

- Sensing minute vibrations indicating that a piece of equipment or a structure is nearing the point of failure and needs to be repaired or replaced. This would prevent catastrophes involving major infrastructure such as bridges and oil refineries.

- Detecting and quantifying explosive materials and toxic substances such as mercury, lead, melamine, and sarin—all at levels low enough to make averting major incidents possible.

- Identifying infectious biological agents, such as *E. coli* and salmonella, to prevent them from entering the food chain.

Such monitoring would help us prevent waste and avoid tragedies that cost lives, impair health, damage the ecosystem, or require a fortune to redress. Our goal at the Information and Quantum Systems Laboratory at Hewlett-Packard is to build what we call a central nervous system for the earth (CeNSE) by *literally instrumenting the planet.*

Reaching this long-term goal depends on our addressing a host of significant challenges: data handling and storage on a gigantic scale; a workable process and tools for continuous monitoring and analysis; a means of routing automatic alerts—including relevant background information—when threshold conditions are exceeded anywhere in the system; and a resilient networking and computing fabric that can absorb and recover from attacks.

To solve these problems our lab will spend the next several years conducting field trials and pilot projects of our sensor networks in industrial settings that offer scaled-down versions of the complex, highly variable conditions CeNSE will confront once it's deployed globally. Our near-term focus will therefore be on devising large enterprise applications that allow us to share development and engineering costs with like-minded partners.

We expect to find early adopters of these applications in the manufacturing and construction industries, particularly energy production and infrastructure development. Sensor networks will enable plant managers to optimize operations—saving material, energy, and money—and will prevent failures in our transportation network that could compromise safety, health, or environmental quality.

Within four to six years, as the technology matures, costs continue to decline, and we learn from our pilot projects, similar networks could be deployed to monitor watersheds, forests, and the food supply. Within six to 10 years, we expect, economies of scale for sensor systems will enable individuals to be ever more aware and in control of their local environments. For example, low-cost sensors might plug into cell phones and allow consumers to check for pesticide residues on supermarket produce that is falsely labeled organic. Or personal devices might provide secure communications and transactions while protecting their owners' privacy. Empowering people to communicate with the earth directly, through globally dispersed sensor systems, and with one another should encourage individual behavioral changes and drive institutions to make us all better stewards of the planet.

R. STANLEY WILLIAMS is an HP senior fellow and director of the Information and Quantum Systems Laboratory at Hewlett-Packard Labs in Palo Alto, California.